Help Me Find My Painting!

Cindy Prince

Book 1: Edouard Manet

Hi there!

My name is Jean, and I've lost my painting!

One minute, I was listening to a traveling musician in Paris, and the next, I was here!

If I give you clues...

Will you help me find my painting?

I was painted by
Edouard Manet in 1862.
My painting is set in the
French countryside.

**Finding my painting is
going to be tricky.**

Look closely at my shirt.

Do you see how the
colors aren't blended
together?

Instead, the pigments
are sitting side by side!

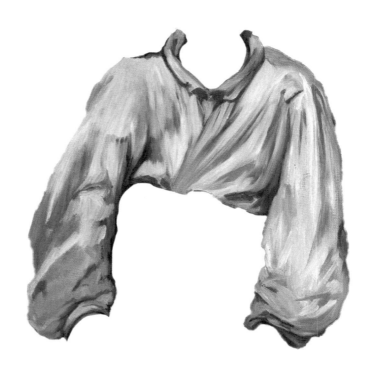

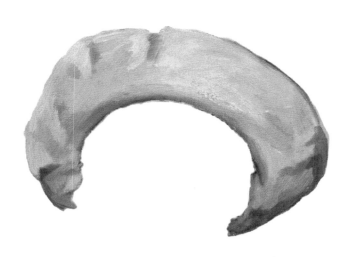

Now look at my hat.

This doesn't look like a *real* hat, does it?

But the colors and brush strokes give you the *impression* of a hat.

You know what it is even if it's not exactly how it looks in real life!

This is called Impressionism!

Do you think you can
find it?

Let's Go!

Is this my painting?

Two Women Chatting By the Sea, St. Thomas

What do you think?

No!

Why not?

Because the colors are blended!

That makes the image too soft to match me!

Is this my painting?

New York

What do you think?

No!

Why not?

This painting is much too modern and busy.

But can you find me on the streets of New York?

Is this my painting?

The House Maid

What do you think?

No!

Why not?

This painting is too real!

Do you see how everything is supposed to look just like it does in real life?

Look at those feathers and the shine on the vases!

Is this my painting?

Oyster Sloop

What do you think?

No!

Why not?

This artist used small strokes of paint to create the image.

Can you see all the different colors in the water?

Is this impressionism?   **Yes!**

We're getting closer!

Is this my painting?

The Old Musician

What do you think?

Yes!

The Old Musician

You helped me find my painting!

The Railway

Edouard Manet

He started drawing when he was very young.

Instead of layering colors on top of each other like other artists, he did something completely different by placing colors next to each other.

He painted normal, every-day scenes where he lived.

Artists change over time as they find new ideas and explore new styles.

Can you see how Manet's brushwork became more free and loose in the next two paintings?

At The Races

Bon Bock Café

Edouard Manet

French, 1832 - 1883

Born in Paris in 1832 to a wealthy family, Édouard Manet showed promise in drawing and caricature from an early age. After twice being denied admission to France's prestigious Naval College, he enrolled in 1850 at the studio of academic artist Thomas Couture. While copying paintings at the Louvre, Manet became attracted to the bold brushwork of Spanish painter Diego Velázquez. He soon adopted a free manner of painting that opposed the polished surfaces revered by academic artists. Rather than gradually building up a composition with layers of blended pigments and translucent glazes, Manet selected and applied patches of color side by side, from the start, for their final effect.

Manet set out on his own artistic career in 1856. Soon after, his focus on modern subject matter – street scenes, bar life, and backhanded versions of famous art icons – coupled with his unconventional paint handling, regularly provoked critics' wrath. Olympia, a painting of a naked courtesan who frankly engages the viewer in parody of the classic Venus, triggered an unparalleled scandal when it was exhibited at the 1865 Salon. The uproar made Manet the de facto leader of the avant-garde.

Manet's bold style, contemporary subject matter, and determination to challenge entrenched academic models influenced younger artists who would come to be known as the impressionists. Manet, too, learned from them, lightening his palette and using even freer brushwork. But he did not share the impressionists' spontaneity; the striking immediacy of Manet's greatest works resulted from a deliberate process involving drawing, models, and painting in a studio. Still determined to make his mark in the official Salon, he declined the more radical option of exhibiting with the impressionists.

Manet continued producing enigmatic and inventive paintings about urban life until his death in 1883. While he had gained a reputation as an influential innovator, only posthumously would he be recognized as a father of modern art.

--The National Gallery of Art

Art Citations

Pissaro, Camille. Two Women Chatting By The Sea, St. Thomas. 1856.
Collection of Mr. and Mrs. Paul Mellon. National Gallery of Art.
https://www.nga.gov/collection/art-object-page.66428.html

Bellows, George. New York. 1911.
Collection of Mr. and Mrs. Paul Mellon. National Gallery of Art.
https://www.nga.gov/collection/art-object-page.69392.html

Hassam, Childe. Oyster Sloop, Cos Cob. 1902.
Ailsa Mellon Bruce Collection. National Gallery of Art.
https://www.nga.gov/collection/art-object-page.52244.html

Paxton, William McGregor. The House Maid. 1910.
Corcoran Collection. National Gallery of Art.
https://www.nga.gov/collection/art-object-page.166466.html

Manet, Edouard. The Old Musician. 1862.
Chester Dale Collection. National Gallery of Art.
https://www.nga.gov/collection/art-object-page.46637.html

Manet, Edouard. The Railway. 1872.
National Gallery of Art.
https://www.nga.gov/collection/art-object-page.43624.html

Manet, Edouard. Bon Bock Café. 1881.
Ailsa Mellon Bruce Collection. National Gallery of Art.
https://www.nga.gov/collection/art-object-page.52182.html

Manet, Edouard. At The Races. 1875.
Widener Collection. National Gallery of Art.
https://www.nga.gov/collection/art-object-page.1180.html

About the Author

Cindy is first and foremost mother to her four beautiful children and wife to her charming and handsome husband, Scott. She is a musician, a gardener, an athlete, an actor, a lover of Canadian chocolate, and most recently, a writer.

Cindy grew up in Airdrie, AB, Canada, but has lived most of her adult life between California and Colorado. She currently resides in the Denver metro area. Cindy graduated from Brigham Young University in 2005 with a B.S. in Psychology, minoring in Business. She serves actively within her church and community and is always up for a new adventure.

After homeschooling for nine years and having countless discussions with her own four children, Cindy decided to start taking notes. Her picture books are inspired by real conversation and interests with the goal of providing stories that are both fun and helpful for families like her own.

@CindyGWrites
www.CindyPrinceAuthor.com